Families Today

INCARCERATION AND FAMILIES

Families Today

Adoptive Families

Disability and Families

Foster Families

Homelessness and Families

Immigrant Families

Incarceration and Families

LGBT Families

Military Families

Multigenerational Families

Multiracial Families

Single-Parent Families

Teen Parents

Families Today

INCARCERATION AND FAMILIES

H.W. Poole

MASON CREST

 3 2401 00909 406 3

Mason Crest
450 Parkway Drive, Suite D
Broomall, PA 19008
www.masoncrest.com

© 2017 by Mason Crest, an imprint of National Highlights, Inc. All rights reserved. No part of this publication may be reproduced or transmitted in any form or by any means, electronic or mechanical, including photocopying, recording, taping, or any information storage and retrieval system, without permission from the publisher.

MTM Publishing, Inc.
435 West 23rd Street, #8C
New York, NY 10011
www.mtmpublishing.com

President: Valerie Tomaselli
Vice President, Book Development: Hilary Poole
Designer: Annemarie Redmond
Copyeditor: Peter Jaskowiak
Editorial Assistant: Andrea St. Aubin

Series ISBN: 978-1-4222-3612-3
Hardback ISBN: 978-1-4222-3618-5
E-Book ISBN: 978-1-4222-8262-5

Library of Congress Cataloging-in-Publication Data
Names: Poole, Hilary W., author.
Title: Incarceration and families / by H.W. Poole.
Description: Broomall, PA : Mason Crest [2017] | Series: Families Today | Includes index.
Identifiers: LCCN 2016004542| ISBN 9781422236185 (hardback) | ISBN 9781422236123 (series) | ISBN 9781422282625 (e-book)
Subjects: LCSH: Prisoners' families—Juvenile literature. | Children of prisoners—Juvenile literature. | Prisoners—Family relationships—Juvenile literature. | Families—Juvenile literature.
Classification: LCC HV8885 .P66 2017 | DDC 362.82/92—dc23
LC record available at http://lccn.loc.gov/2016004542

Printed and bound in the United States of America.

First printing
9 8 7 6 5 4 3 2 1

TABLE OF CONTENTS

Series Introduction 7
Chapter One: Understanding Incarceration 11
Chapter Two: How Did We Get Here? 19
Chapter Three: Parents and Prison 27
Chapter Four: After Release 37
Further Reading 44
Series Glossary 45
Index 47
About the Author 48
Photo Credits 48

Key Icons to Look for:

Words to Understand: These words with their easy-to-understand definitions will increase the reader's understanding of the text, while building vocabulary skills.

Sidebars: This boxed material within the main text allows readers to build knowledge, gain insights, explore possibilities, and broaden their perspectives by weaving together additional information to provide realistic and holistic perspectives.

Research Projects: Readers are pointed toward areas of further inquiry connected to each chapter. Suggestions are provided for projects that encourage deeper research and analysis.

Text-Dependent Questions: These questions send the reader back to the text for more careful attention to the evidence presented there.

Series Glossary of Key Terms: This back-of-the-book glossary contains terminology used throughout the series. Words found here increase the reader's ability to read and comprehend higher-level books and articles in this field.

In the 21st century, families are more diverse than ever before.

SERIES INTRODUCTION

Our vision of "the traditional family" is not nearly as time-honored as one might think. The standard of a mom, a dad, and a couple of kids in a nice house with a white-picket fence is a relic of the 1950s—the heart of the baby boom era. The tumult of the Great Depression followed by a global war caused many Americans to long for safety and predictability—whether such stability was real or not. A newborn mass media was more than happy to serve up this image, in the form of TV shows like *Leave It To Beaver* and *The Adventures of Ozzie and Harriet*. Interestingly, even back in the "glory days" of the traditional family, things were never as simple as they seemed. For example, a number of the classic "traditional" family shows—such as *The Andy Griffith Show, My Three Sons,* and a bit later, *The Courtship of Eddie's Father*—were actually focused on single-parent families.

Sure enough, by the 1960s our image of the "perfect family" was already beginning to fray at the seams. The women's movement, the gay rights movement, and—perhaps more than any single factor—the advent of "no fault" divorce meant that the illusion of the Cleaver family would become harder and harder to maintain. By the early 21st century, only about 7 percent of all family households were traditional—defined as a married couple with children where *only* the father works outside the home.

As the number of these traditional families has declined, "nontraditional" arrangements have increased. There are more single parents, more gay and lesbian parents, and more grandparents raising grandchildren than ever before. Multiracial families—created either through interracial relationships or adoption—are also increasing. Meanwhile, the transition to an all-volunteer military force has meant that there are more kids growing up in military families than there were in the past. Each of these topics is treated in a separate volume in this set.

While some commentators bemoan the decline of the traditional family, others argue that, overall, the recognition of new family arrangements has brought more good than bad. After all, if very few people live like the Cleavers anyway, isn't it better to be honest about that fact? Surely, holding up the traditional family as an ideal to which all should aspire only serves to stigmatize kids whose lives differ from that standard. After all, no children can be held responsible for whatever family they find themselves in; all they can do is grow up as best they can. These books take the position that every family—no matter what it looks like—has the potential to be a successful family.

That being said, challenges and difficulties arise in every family, and nontraditional ones are no exception. For example, single parents tend to be less well off financially than married parents are, and this has long-term impacts on their children. Meanwhile, teenagers who become parents tend to let their educations suffer, which damages their income potential and career possibilities, as well as risking the future educational attainment of their babies. There are some 400,000 children in the foster care system at any given time. We know that the uncertainty of foster care creates real challenges when it comes to both education and emotional health.

Furthermore, some types of "nontraditional" families are ones we wish did not have to exist at all. For example, an estimated 1.6 million children experience homelessness at some point in their lives. At least 40 percent of homeless kids are lesbian, gay, bisexual, or transgender teens who were turned out of their homes because of their orientation. Meanwhile, the United States incarcerates more people than any other nation in the world—about 2.7 million kids (1 in 28) have an incarcerated parent. It would be absurd to pretend that such situations are not extremely stressful and, often, detrimental to kids who have to survive them.

The goal of this set, then, is twofold. First, we've tried to describe the history and shape of various nontraditional families in such a way that kids who aren't familiar with them will be able to not only understand, but empathize. We also present demographic information that may be useful for students who are dipping their toes into introductory sociology concepts.

Second, we have tried to speak specifically to the young people who are living in these nontraditional families. The series strives to address these kids as

Meeting challenges and overcoming them together can make families stronger.

sympathetically and supportively as possible. The volumes look at some of the typical problems that kids in these situations face, and where appropriate, they offer advice and tips for how these kids might get along better in whatever situation confronts them.

Obviously, no single book—whether on disability, the military, divorce, or some other topic—can hope to answer every question or address every problem. To that end, a "Further Reading" section at the back of each book attempts to offer some places to look next. We have also listed appropriate crisis hotlines, for anyone with a need more immediate than can be addressed by a library.

Whether your students have a project to complete or a problem to solve, we hope they will be able to find clear, empathic information about nontraditional families in these pages.

—H. W. Poole

10 Incarceration and Families

Experts describe incarceration as "a series of crises" that begins with the arrest.

Chapter One

UNDERSTANDING INCARCERATION

The word *family* has had many meanings over the years. Even today, it means different things to different people. Keeping things as simple as possible, you might define a family as "people who are there for you." A lot of times those people are related by biology, but they can also be your "family by choice." Either way, they are the people who stick with you through the good times and the bad times. They are the ones who love you and forgive you, even when you make a mistake.

Words to Understand

anxiety: a feeling of worry or nervousness.

bail: the money that an arrested person pays to be released from jail while waiting for trial.

depression: severe sadness or unhappiness that does not go away easily.

incarceration: being confined in prison or jail.

traumatic: something that's very disturbing and causes long-term damage to a person.

variable: something that can change.

Incarceration and Families

But what if someone in your family makes a really big mistake? And what if he or she has to pay for that mistake by spending time in prison? That's the kind of mistake that is going to have a huge impact on the whole family.

UNDERSTANDING THE TERMS

People often use the words *prison* and *jail* as though they mean the same thing. But actually they are quite different. The United States has more than 3,200 jails and 1,800 prisons. Jails are run by local authorities, such as town or city governments. People who have been arrested and are awaiting trial are held in jail, not in prison. In many places, people who are serving short sentences (usually less than one year) are also held in jail.

Prisons, on the other hand, are for people serving longer sentences for more serious crimes. Prisons are run by either state or federal authorities. Whether

An arrest can affect the whole family, not just the person who was arrested.

Chapter One: Understanding Incarceration   13

Encounters with police can be scary for little kids, even in situations where the officer is just trying to help.

someone goes to state or federal prison is determined mostly by what type of crime was committed. There are also several different types of prison, including minimum security and maximum security facilities. Prisoners in a minimum security facility have usually committed less serious crimes, and they have more freedom of movement within the prison.

CRISIS AFTER CRISIS

Like the concept of family, the concept of **incarceration** is more complicated than it sounds. Sometimes the experience of incarceration is described as "a series of crises." Every situation is different, but in general it goes like this: there is an arrest, there is a wait for a trial (or plea deal), and then there is the trial (or plea deal). If the person is convicted, he or she is sentenced, meaning that a judge or

Understanding the Numbers

The distinction between jails and prisons, combined with the distinction between state and federal facilities, can make it difficult to get precise statistics. Some researchers keep state and federal numbers separate, while others combine the two. Some include jails, while some don't. This is why, for example, you might hear that just over a million kids have parents in prison, or you might hear that the number is closer to 3 million. This is because of differences in the way the term *prison* was defined by the researchers.

Another issue is that prisoners often change status or get moved around. After all, a lot of people being held in jail have not been convicted of anything—they are in jail waiting for trial. Nearly 12 million people go through the local jail system every year. Researchers call this uncertainty "jail churn." Jail churn makes it tricky to get an accurate picture of how many people are being held at any given time. In 2014 the group Prison Policy Initiative put together a breakdown of different types of facilities, based on data from 2011. The following list shows the number of inmates in the various types of facilities in the United States:

- state prisons: 1,362,028
- federal prisons: 216,362
- local jails: 721,654 (awaiting trial: 428,312; serving a jail sentence: 293,342)
- juvenile facilities: 70,792
- immigration detention: 34,000
- territorial* prisons: 13,576
- civil commitment: 5,640
- military prison: 1,434
- Indian country jails: 2,146

*Meaning U.S. territories such as Puerto Rico.
Source: Prison Policy Initiative. www.prisonpolicy.org/reports/pie.html.

Chapter One: Understanding Incarceration

jury decides how long the person will have to be incarcerated. That's followed by the period of incarceration, and then, if all goes well, a return to freedom. All of these points present different challenges and, too often, **traumatic** moments for the arrested person's children.

For many kids, the experience of seeing their mom or dad arrested is very traumatic. In one survey of kids who were present when their parents got arrested, 70 percent saw the police handcuff their parent. About 30 percent had guns drawn on them. Sometimes kids are left alone in the house after their parent is taken to jail. Other times, the kids are taken away, as well—either by police or social workers. Many kids end up feeling like *they* were the ones who got arrested. It is common for kids to feel **anxiety** or **depression**, and to have nightmares, even after the arrest is over.

The arrest of a parent can have a big impact on a child's feelings about law enforcement. If police officers burst into your home and frighten you, or if you watch as they take your parent away, you might have a pretty negative view of the police. Obviously, police have to do their jobs, and that may involve bursting into a house sometimes. But using sensitivity when dealing with children makes long-term sense. Michael Hennessey, a sheriff in San Francisco, notes, "If children are abused by the criminal justice system, they will have hostility towards law enforcement as adults. If they are treated fairly, and see government as a place to receive assistance as opposed to something that takes away rights, they will be more likely to reach out to and respect government as adults."

After the arrest, there is a period of uncertainty. Will the parent be able to pay **bail** and come home until the trial? If not, where will the kids live in the meantime? This pretrial period can be over in a short time, or it can stretch on for months or even years. You can imagine how stressful this is for kids, who have no control over what happens next.

If the parent is convicted, then there is a period of incarceration, and finally reentry into society. The last part, coming home, is supposed to be "the good

Incarceration and Families

part," but it can also cause a crisis in the family. (See chapter four for more on this.) These "crises" all create different challenges for families.

There are other **variables**, too, such as the length of the sentence. The distance between prison and the family's home is another important factor. Incarceration is thus not just one general experience—it's many different ones. Which family member is in prison also has a huge impact on the rest of the family. That is, it's one type of experience to have a father in prison, but it is a very different type of experience to have a mother in prison. Neither is "better" or "worse" than the other—they are just different.

KIDS IN JAIL

The United States is not only the world's top jailer of adults, but also of young people. Between 60,000 and 70,000 people under age 18 are incarcerated on any

Most of the time, juvenile cases are handled by a separate court from adult cases.

Chapter One: Understanding Incarceration

given day. The majority of these kids are being held for what experts call "minor offenses," including skipping school or running away from home.

The somewhat good news is that the overall totals have been declining in recent years. After increasing steadily every year from 1979 to 1987, the rate has been dropping ever since. The bad news is that increasing numbers of teenagers are being sent to adult facilities, and reports of prisoner abuse are increasing.

Unfortunately, the issue of incarcerated kids is too big to be addressed in this short book. However, many of the issues discussed in chapter three, about the impact of incarcerated parents on kids, also apply to kids who have a brother or sister in jail. See also the sidebar on page 34, which gives advice on how to cope when a family member is locked up. Those tips apply just as well to siblings, too.

Text-Dependent Questions

1. What is the general pattern of events after someone is arrested?
2. Why can arrests be traumatic for kids?
3. How many people under the age of 18 are incarcerated on any given day?

Research Project

Find out about a jail that is located in your community and compare it to a prison in your state. Write up a table comparing both, including columns for where each are located, who runs each, how many employees they have, how many people are incarcerated in each, and so forth.

18 Incarceration and Families

Outside the Eastern State Penitentiary in Pennsylvania.

Chapter Two

HOW DID WE GET HERE?

Through much of the 20th century, the rate of incarceration in the United States was roughly 100 prisoners per 100,000 people. In the 1980s, however, things began to change. A "war on drugs" was declared, causing a spike in arrests for drug-related crimes. A trend toward **mandatory** sentencing meant that judges had no option but to give out the harshest possible punishments. Some states got rid of **parole** for many offenses. Since the 1980s, the number of prisoners has consistently gone up. In 2015 the rate was 500 people in prison per 100,000. And if you

Words to Understand

confinement: the state of being locked up or restrained.

corporal: physical, involving the body.

disparity: a noticeable difference between two things.

mandatory: required.

parole: the state of being let out of prison early, to serve the rest of the sentence in the outside world.

psychological: having to do with the mind.

combine both prison and jail, the rate was 700 per 100,000 people. This means that United States has more prisoners than any country in the world—even more than North Korea, Russia, or Iran.

THE ORIGIN OF U.S. PRISONS

Prisons were invented in the 1780s, at about the same time the United States was born. Jails have been around since ancient times, but they only held people for short periods. When someone was accused of a crime, he only stayed in jail until he'd been convicted and punished in some other way. Punishments usually involved fines or some form of **corporal** punishment. For example, a thief might have paid a fine and been whipped.

American prisons were a reaction against the workhouses that existed in Europe at that time. Workhouses were a bit like jails, but they used physical punishment and hard labor. **Confinement** in the workhouse was not viewed as the true punishment—being forced to break rocks was the punishment. The confinement was a secondary concern.

One big problem with workhouses was that everyone who'd been charged with a crime—male or female, adult or child, violent or nonviolent—got confined together. Guards were not responsible for keeping prisoners safe, and there were no clear rules about how they should treat prisoners. Reformers became very worried about the violence and abuse that was taking place behind the walls of the workhouse.

What's a Penitentiary?

The religious roots of our prison system can be seen in the word *penitentiary*, which is just another word for a prison. The word comes from *penitence*, which is the religious concept of shame or guilt for bad behavior.

Chapter Two: How Did We Get Here?

Sing Sing Prison in Ossining, New York.

The American Revolution may have started over taxes and tea, but it quickly became a rejection of all things British—and that included the British justice system. The religious group called the Quakers, who founded Pennsylvania and had many members throughout the new country, objected to corporal punishment. They argued that forced confinement was a more humane method of handling crime. This idea led to the creation of the American prison.

For a long time, America had two types of prisons. One was called the *solitary system*. First created at the Eastern State Penitentiary in Pennsylvania, the solitary system was pretty much what it sounds like—prisoners were kept alone in individual cells and rarely interacted with anyone else. Each cell had its own skylight, running water, toilet, and private outside yard. The idea was to encourage prisoners to reflect on their crimes. Prisoners even had to wear hoods when being taken from place to place—this was to shield them from "distractions."

Incarceration and Families

Case Study: Philip and Dorothy

Philip remembers the moment his mother Dorothy walked out of the prison. He rubbed his eyes, barely able to believe it was her. At one time, Dorothy was a hard-working, churchgoing nurse technician. But she was convicted of dealing drugs when Philip was 9 years old. When she got out, he was 16, and a troublesome teenager. He had been an honor student when his mother went to prison, but he had a rough time without her. Philip failed the eighth grade three times.

Now Dorothy found herself homeless and unable to get work in nursing. Philip could only watch as Dorothy became more bitter and frustrated. "She was there physically, but mentally she wasn't," Philip says. "It's like she's still incarcerated. Her mind is somewhere else."

Although he was happy to have his mother home, Philip also had a lot of feelings he didn't know what to do with. Suddenly he was angry with his mother all the time—much angrier than he'd ever felt when she was away. They fought frequently. As time passed, though, he came to understand the difficult situation in which Dorothy found herself. "People think that you can just come out and jump back in; that life has left a space open for you. There is not a space open for my mother. There is not a place for her."

—Based on a story in *All Alone in the World: Children of the Incarcerated*, by Nell Bernstein.

The second system was called the *congregate system*. It began with two prisons in New York State: Auburn and Sing Sing. To "congregate" means to gather together. In these facilities, prisoners lived, ate, and worked together. But there was a catch: they were expected to be completely silent all the time.

Each system had its admirers and critics, but the congregate system became increasingly popular. For one thing, many people had concerns about the

psychological impact of the solitary system (see below). Also—and perhaps more importantly—the solitary system was extremely expensive. For instance, each prisoner in Eastern State Penitentiary had his own faucet at a time when even the White House did not have running water. By the 1920s, even the Eastern State Penitentiary had abandoned the solitary system.

CRITIQUES OF THE PRISON SYSTEM

In the 19th century, European visitors toured American prisons and brought the ideas that informed them back to use in their home countries. The French writers Alexis de Tocqueville and Gustave de Beaumont praised the solitary system in the 1830s. In fact, hundreds of prisons were built all over the world based on the one in Pennsylvania. But when the British author Charles Dickens visited a solitary system prison, he was horrified by what he saw. He wrote,

I believe [solitary confinement], in its effects, to be cruel and wrong.... I believe that very few men are capable of estimating the immense amount of torture and agony which this dreadful punishment, prolonged for years, inflicts upon the sufferers.... I hold this slow and daily tampering with the mysteries of the brain to be immeasurably worse than any torture of the body.

Charles Dickens.

Incarceration and Families

Dickens's arguments against solitary confinement are still made to this day.

In fact, critiques of the prison system have been around for a very long time. Consider, for example, modern discussions about racial **disparity** in prisons. A white American man has less than a 1 in 10 chance of being imprisoned at some point in his life. But an African American man has a 1 in 3 chance.

This situation is not new. In 1814, for example, 29 percent of the men in New York state prisons were black, even though black people in general made up a far smaller percentage of the population. After the Civil War, 75 percent of the inmates of prisons in southern states were black men. This led some observers at

What's Old Is New Again

Recently, an old question became the topic of a new debate: What is the connection between America's history of discrimination against African Americans and the current trends in incarceration? It is a complicated question with no easy answers.

Two important articles from 2015 outline the opposite sides of this debate. In "The Black Family in the Age of Mass Incarceration," Ta-Nehisi Coates points out that the simple desire to be free was illegal for slaves. In effect, he argues, black Americans have often been viewed as "criminal," just because natural human instincts were criminalized. This history, Coates said, makes it far too easy for people to believe that blacks are more inclined toward crime.

On the other side, in the essay "The Truth about Mass Incarceration" Stephanos Bibas denies there is a racial bias in imprisonment. Bibas points instead to increases in crime and stricter policing. But Coates and Bibas agree that America's prison system is in trouble. These essays are long and written at a high level, but they are worth a look if you are interested in this issue. Both are listed in the "Further Reading" section at the back of this book.

Chapter Two: How Did We Get Here?

the time to say that prisons were being used as a replacement for slavery. In the 21st century, when 1 in 15 African Americans is incarcerated, some people still find this argument persuasive, while others do not (see sidebar).

Text-Dependent Questions

1. What is the rate of incarceration in the United States?
2. What were the two original types of prisons?
3. What are some of the criticisms that have been made of the U.S. system?

Research Project

Find out more about incarceration around the world. What countries incarcerate the most people? Which ones incarcerate the least? Why? You might start with the country profiles posted on the website of the Institute for Criminal Policy Research, available at http://www.prisonstudies.org/world-prison-brief.

26 Incarceration and Families

Telling kids the truth about having to go to prison can be very hard.

Chapter Three

PARENTS IN PRISON

Parents facing prison time have to figure out how and what to tell their kids. It's common to feel shame when someone goes to prison. Parents might not want to talk about it. Plus, they don't want their kids to worry. Sometimes it might seem easier to just not tell the kids. This is especially true when it comes to fathers who don't live with their children. A mom might say something like, "Your father is away for work." And that might actually sound believable if the kids don't expect to see their dad every day, anyhow.

Words to Understand

commissary: a store on a military base or prison that sells food and other items.

debt: something that's owed; in this case, money owed to credit card companies and other businesses.

stigma: a judgment that something is bad or shameful.

stress: an emotion involving tension and fear.

Incarceration and Families

But the truth has a way of coming out. First of all, kids tend to have good instincts for when their parents are upset. Also, they're likely to hear about the incarceration from relatives, friends, or people in the neighborhood. They might see a piece of mail from the prison, or they might overhear someone talking about the situation on the phone. Once the secret gets out, the kids will be angry—and for good reason. Catching a parent in a lie that big can cause kids to have trouble trusting adults in the future.

Also, if the truth is kept from them, kids may invent their own reasons to explain a parent's disappearance. Often, those made-up stories will involve blaming themselves. For all these reasons, experts say that, as uncomfortable as the situation is, honesty really is the best policy.

Although it's the parent who has been convicted and the parent who is jailed, the impact of that situation touches everyone else in the family. A few of the key issues are discussed in this chapter.

IMPACT ON FINANCES

There's an old saying that "crime pays." But for people who get arrested, it's actually pretty expensive. There are lawyer fees and court fees, which the convicted person will have to pay. But when a person in jail has no income, the family gets the bill. One study found that the families of convicts ended up paying these fees about 63 percent of the time. And among families who had a family member convicted of a crime, 48 percent couldn't afford the costs. The result of all this is **debt**. The average family debt for court costs is over $13,000.

The costs don't end after the conviction. A simple phone conversation can be expensive (see box on page 30). When people in prison need anything, from soap to writing paper, it has to be purchased from the **commissary**. Although many prisoners do work while incarcerated, the pay is extremely low—often just a few cents per hour. The result is that many prisoners do not earn enough

Chapter Three: Parents in Prison

The unincarcerated parent often bears a heavy financial burden.

money to pay for their own purchases from the commissary, never mind contributing to their family's budget.

Then there are visits. Studies have proven the importance of prisoners remaining connected to their loved ones on the outside. It's pretty easy to understand why. The more prisoners stay focused on their families, the more likely they are to avoid trouble while they are inside. Prisoners who have lost contact with the outside world may feel that they have less to lose. But families frequently have to make long drives, or even fly, in order to visit their incarcerated loved one. This means missing work and paying for gasoline, airfare, or bus tickets. The result is even more debt. A study by the Ella Baker Center for Human Rights found that 34 percent of families went into debt due to phone calls and visits alone.

Incarceration and Families

Prison Phone Calls

People who study incarceration agree that keeping in touch with "the outside" is important. Maintaining relationships with family members helps prisoners stay focused on getting out. It also means that the prisoners will have somewhere to go when they do get out. So you would think that helping prisoners communicate with their families would be a high priority for every prison and jail. But when it comes to phone calls, that doesn't seem to be true.

Rates for prison phone calls vary. But they are almost always much more expensive than regular calls—as high as $17 per 15-minute call. In one situation covered by the *New York Times*, a 15-minute call cost $12.95, but that was just the beginning of the charges. There was a $6.95 fee charged every time someone put money into the prisoner's phone account. So, for example, if $25 was deposited, the prisoner only got $18.05 worth of calling time. There's also a monthly fee for having the account, and another fee for each call made. Sometimes there's even a fee for providing a refund if there is money left in the account when the person gets out.

Fortunately, in 2015 the Federal Communications Commission (FCC) passed new rules about the how much companies can charge. But advocates continue to push the FCC to make phoning home fair and affordable.

Payphones at a prison in Philadelphia.

Chapter Three: Parents in Prison

The people who are most affected are the ones least able to afford it. Two out of three families reported having trouble paying their bills while their loved one was incarcerated. Just under half of the families surveyed had trouble buying food and paying for housing.

IMPACTS ON PARTNERS

For the vast majority of kids, their father is the one serving time. When fathers are sent to jail or prison, mothers usually take care of their kids on their own. In one survey by the Bureau of Justice Statistics (BJS), about 88 percent of kids whose fathers were incarcerated were being cared for by their mothers. Other arrangements involved grandparents, other relatives, friends, or foster homes.

Of course, many of these women were single moms to begin with. That is, they were taking care of their kids on their own already. But even if the parents

Visiting a prison can be intimidating, in part due to the tight security.

were not living together, the father could still spend time with his kids. He could still earn money to help take care of them. Once he has to go to prison, that stops. As mentioned above, prisoners can and do have jobs, but the pay is extremely low. This creates a lot of **stress** for the parent who is "on the outside" taking care of the kids.

It's natural for parents to feel frustrated that they are left handling "real life" while their partners are incarcerated. Some find that their friends or family members start to pull away a bit, due to the social **stigma** attached to being incarcerated. Unfortunately, incarceration is associated with an increased chance of divorce (or breakup, if the parents are not married). Sometimes mothers are inclined to go on with their lives. A mother may want to start a relationship with someone new, rather than wait for a father to get out of prison. According to a study called "Fragile Families and Child Well-Being," incarceration makes it more likely that couples will split up within one year of the prisoner's release.

IMPACTS ON KIDS

When a family has financial problems, it affects everybody. If there's no money for food or rent, that hurts the kids as much as the adults. But for many kids with incarcerated parents, money is not really the first thing on their minds. The absence of their parent has the biggest impact. Kids can feel sad, scared, and even angry about the fact that their parent is incarcerated. They may feel ashamed, and they may get teased by kids at school. Having an incarcerated parent means kids are more likely to suffer from anxiety and depression. They are more likely to "act out" and get in trouble at school.

Young kids, especially, tend to assume that the incarceration is somehow their fault. They need a lot of reassurance that their parents love them and will always love them. They need to understand that whatever caused the incarceration had nothing to do with them.

Chapter Three: Parents in Prison

Having a parent in prison can cause kids to be anxious or depressed. Sometimes they get teased or bullied, too.

Kids will probably also worry about their parent's safety. Visits can be great for easing some of these concerns. Even though prison can be a scary place, if kids see where their parents are, that can help ease their minds. It helps to see their parents with their own eyes, so they know they are okay. But as touched on above, visits are often difficult, and they are sometimes impossible to manage.

According to ABC News, the majority of prisoners are held far from home. About 62 percent of state prisoners and 84 percent of federal prisoners are incarcerated more than 100 miles from where they live. Plus, prisons are almost never directly connected to public transportation like buses and trains. This makes it challenging for families to visit their loved ones. Letters, phone calls, and (where possible) video chats are other ways of staying in touch. But those can be expensive, too (see box on page 30).

Incarceration and Families

Coping Tips

The Virginia-based group Assisting Families of Inmates offers services to families who are dealing with incarceration. Some of the families they work with created a list of tips to help other families cope with this difficult situation. Here are a few pieces of advice from them:

- Don't blame yourself. You aren't responsible for what your family member did.
- Don't put your own life on hold. It's hard, but you need to keep going with your own plans and dreams.
- Do maintain relationships with other friends and family members. Look for support groups in your community, where you can meet other families who are going through similar struggles.
- Do continue your family traditions and celebrations. Look for creative ways to include your loved one who is incarcerated, but don't give up on the celebrations just because that person can't be there.

MOTHERS IN PRISON

The vast majority of prisoners are male—in 2015, only 6.7 percent of prisoners were women. But just because it's a small percentage, that doesn't mean it's a small number—it's still more than 100,000 women. More than a few of these women are mothers. Most incarcerated fathers can count on mothers to take care of the kids, but the reverse is not always true. Only 37 percent of incarcerated mothers have partners on the outside who take care of their kids. The rest depend on other family members (especially grandparents) and, sometimes, foster care.

One big question is what to do about babies. As many as 1 in 25 women in state prisons, and 1 in 33 women in federal prisons, are pregnant when they are sentenced. What happens when they give birth, and what happens to the babies afterwards? This is not a happy situation. First, it is legal in 37 states to shackle a female prisoner while she gives birth. The majority of the time, babies are separated from their mothers immediately afterward. If there is no family member who can take care of the infant, the baby will end up in foster care.

But a small number of states, including Illinois, New York, Ohio, and West Virginia, have nurseries in their women's prisons. A prison nursery is supposed to help mother and baby bond with each other. This will make mother and child more likely to stay connected later. Keeping a mother and baby together in a prison is very expensive, however. Some estimates put the cost as high as $24,000 per year. Advocates say that it is wiser to spend that money in the beginning, to help improve the mother–child relationship. Without that support, even more money might be spent later when a poorly raised child grows up to commit crimes, too.

Text-Dependent Questions

1. What are some of the psychological impacts on families of incarcerated people?
2. What usually happens to babies who are born to women in prison?
3. What are some tips to help people cope while a loved one is incarcerated?

Research Project

Look up more pieces of advice for people with incarcerated loved ones. Visit the website of Assisting Families of Inmates (www.afoi.org), as well as the other sites listed in the back of this book. Write up a longer list of tips, and feel free to add any ideas that you might have on your own. Design a poster that highlights the best suggestions.

36 Incarceration and Families

Some people have to wear ankle monitors as a condition of their parole.

Chapter Four

AFTER RELEASE

Sooner or later, most people who've been convicted of crimes will complete their punishment and be let out. Sometimes they have finished the entire sentence and are completely free. More often, however, they are released on some form of **parole**. That usually means they have to check in with a parole officer on a regular basis. People who are "out on probation" have to be very careful not to break any laws or violate the conditions of their release.

Having a parent come home from prison can be a joyful experience. But it can also be a pretty strange one. For one thing, kids get used to *not* having their parent around. When the parent is released, suddenly there is another adult there, with lots of opinions on what the kids should and shouldn't do.

Words to Understand

felony: a crime that is viewed as very serious.

grant: money that is given to individuals or groups to help start a business or other endeavor.

overt: obvious, not hidden.

parole: a conditional release from prison, in which the convicted person is responsible for following a certain list of rules.

restrictions: limits on what someone can do.

Also, people often change while they are incarcerated. *How* they change depends a lot on their personality and what their prison experience was like. Sometimes people become tougher, or "harder," in prison because it's such a difficult environment. People in prison may need to be constantly "on guard" against conflict and violence; this can have a long-lasting effect. There is also what some people call "learned helplessness." People in prison are told what to do and when to do it. They are told what to eat, what to wear, when to sleep, and when to wake up. After many years in this environment, being released into a world of choices can be hard.

A person who has just gotten out of prison might be more short-tempered than you remember. He or she might get frustrated more easily than they did before. On the other hand, some people become more grateful for the "little things" in life once they are out. Some people become more religious in prison, too. It's impossible to predict how prison will affect a specific person—only that it will.

RESTRICTIONS

If someone is convicted of a **felony**, certain things will be very different when he or she gets out. This is because of the way we view convicts in the United States. Chapter one had a little information about the history of incarceration in this country. In colonial times, punishment began and ended fairly quickly. Maybe the convicted person paid a fine, or maybe he was whipped. But whatever the punishment was, once it happened, it was over. People did not view the conviction as a permanent mark on the individual. Things are different now.

When people are convicted of felonies, their convictions will haunt them long after they're released. Legal **restrictions** are placed on convicted felons at the local, state, and federal levels. They include limitations on:
- the ability to vote
- the ability to travel

Chapter Four: After Release

- access to education
- access to public housing
- access to food stamps
- parental rights
- the ability to work in many fields

According to a report from the Ella Baker Center for Human Rights, there are more than 44,000 restrictions on felons in the United States. The nature of the restrictions varies a lot by state. For example, in many states, incarcerated people are not allowed to vote, but their vote is restored once they are out. Other states, such as Florida, do not allow people with felony convictions to vote again at all.

Many employers hold people's criminal records against them during the hiring process.

Incarceration and Families

Some Positives

It would be wrong to pretend that a father going to prison is a good thing. It's not at all. However, in certain situations, there may be positive things that could come out of the situation. Here are some examples:

- If the dad had a tendency to be violent, kids do sometimes feel like life improves when he is no longer in the home.
- If the father had problems with drugs or alcohol, he might be able to get treatment while in prison and get the problem under control.
- Some prisoners view their sentences as opportunities to turn their lives around. They might use their prison time to reflect, to get treatment, or even to take a parenting class. If a father chooses to view his situation that way, it is possible that he can come out as a better person and father.

Some people become more religious when they are incarcerated; sometimes their faith can be very helpful during the hard times after they are released.

Chapter Four: After Release

It may not be easy, but your family *can* build a new life together after the incarceration period is over.

Restrictions like these are **overt**, meaning they are written down and clearly stated. People with felony convictions may not apply for public housing, for example. According to the Welfare Reform Act of 1996, people with felony drug convictions are permanently barred from receiving food stamps. Other restrictions are less overt but still real. For instance, employers are allowed to discriminate against people with convictions when hiring new employees. To many employers, a felony conviction is a "red flag" that will influence them to not hire a person.

One important thing to notice about these restrictions is that people with convictions are kept out of the social programs that are designed to help people in poverty. We have seen in this book how incarceration has a devastating impact on the financial life of a family. The restrictions that haunt

Incarceration and Families

> ## Getting Help
>
> In addition to the organizations mentioned in the text, there are many other governmental and private groups that try to help recently released people. Here are just a few:
> - Anti-Recidivism Coalition (http://www.antirecidivism.org)
> - Center for Employment Opportunities (http://ceoworks.org)
> - Hope After Prison (http://www.hopeafterprison.com/)
> - National Reentry Resource Center (https://csgjusticecenter.org/jc/category/reentry/nrrc)

people with felonies make this situation even worse. Reformers argue that adjusting these restrictions would be a huge step toward helping the families of incarcerated people.

MOVING FORWARD

Rebuilding a family after incarceration is extremely challenging. But things are getting better. And there are many organizations, both private and public, that can help.

Much of the assistance comes from private charities and churches. For example, a program in Kentucky called R6 Ministries helps connect recently released people with mentors. In New Orleans, an organization called The First 72+ is run by former convicts. They have made it their mission to help recently released people get back on their feet. (If someone in your family needs help from an organization like this, try searching on the Internet for "help for convicts" in your state or city.)

Some government agencies offer **grants** to help people start businesses or new careers. The Small Business Administration, the National Endowment for the

Humanities, and the Department of Agriculture all have assistance programs for people with felony convictions who want to start businesses. The privately run Prison Entrepreneurship Program (PEP) offers courses and workshops to help newly released people restart their careers.

There are also companies described as "felony friendly," because they have expressed a willingness to hire people with convictions. Tax benefits for those willing to hire people with felony convictions can help shape such companies hiring policies. A campaign called "Ban the Box," which is a reference to the box you have to check on a job application if you have been in prison, is working to encourage more companies to open up their hiring. Major cities in Connecticut, such as Bridgeport and New Haven, have removed questions about incarceration from applications for city jobs. In late 2015, President Barack Obama announced that the "box" would be banned from applications for federal jobs.

Text-Dependent Questions

1. What kinds of restrictions are placed on people with felony convictions?
2. Why is it sometimes hard on kids when their parent is released?
3. What are some types of help that people can get after they are released?

Research Project

Do a short report on an organization that helps people who have been released from prison. You can select one mentioned in this chapter, or find another on your own. Include three sections: (1) an introduction that describes the way in which the organization helps people with felony convictions, (2) a brief history, and (3) information on the influence the organization has on the people it serves.

Incarceration and Families

FURTHER READING

Books and Articles

Bernstein, Nell. *All Alone in the World: Children of the Incarcerated*. New York: New Press, 2005.

Bibas, Stephanos. "The Truth about Mass Incarceration." *National Review*, September 21, 2015. http://www.nationalreview.com/article/424059/mass-incarceration-prison-reform.

Coates, Ta-Nehisi. "The Black Family in the Age of Mass Incarceration." *The Atlantic*, October 2015. http://www.theatlantic.com/magazine/archive/2015/10/the-black-family-in-the-age-of-mass-incarceration/403246/.

Spanne, Autumn, Nora McCarthy, and Laura Longhine, eds. *Wish You Were Here: Teens Write about Parents in Prison*. New York: Youth Communications, 2010.

Online

Assisting Families of Inmates. www.afoi.org.

Center for Children of Incarcerated Parents. www.e-ccip.org.

National Resource Center on Children and Families of the Incarcerated. http://nrccfi.camden.rutgers.edu/resources/library/children-of-prisoners-library/.

The Sentencing Project. www.sentencingproject.org.

Get Help Now

Childhelp National Child Abuse Hotline

This free hotline is available 24-hours-a-day in 170 different languages.

1-800-4-A-CHILD (1-800-422-4453)   http://www.childhelp.org

SERIES GLOSSARY

agencies: departments of a government with responsibilities for specific programs.

anxiety: a feeling of worry or nervousness.

biological parents: the woman and man who create a child; they may or not raise it.

caregiving: helping someone with their daily activities.

cognitive: having to do with thinking or understanding.

consensus: agreement among a particular group of people.

custody: legal guardianship of a child.

demographers: people who study information about people and communities.

depression: severe sadness or unhappiness that does not go away easily.

discrimination: singling out a group for unfair treatment.

disparity: a noticeable difference between two things.

diverse: having variety; for example, "ethnically diverse" means a group of people of many different ethnicities.

ethnicity: a group that has a shared cultural heritage.

extended family: the kind of family that includes members beyond just parents and children, such as aunts, uncles, cousins, and so on.

foster care: raising a child (usually temporarily) that is not adopted or biologically yours.

heir: someone who receives another person's wealth and social position after the other person dies.

homogenous: a group of things that are the same.

ideology: a set of ideas and ways of seeing the world.

incarceration: being confined in prison or jail.

inclusive: accepting of everyone.

informally: not official or legal.

Incarceration and Families

institution: an established organization, custom, or tradition.

kinship: family relations.

neglect: not caring for something correctly.

patriarchal: a system that is run by men and fathers.

prejudice: beliefs about a person or group based only on simplified and often mistaken ideas.

prevalence: how common a particular trait is in a group of people.

psychological: having to do with the mind.

quantify: to count or measure objectively.

restrictions: limits on what someone can do.

reunification: putting something back together.

secular: nonreligious.

security: being free from danger.

social worker: a person whose job is to help families or children deal with particular problems.

socioeconomic: relating to both social factors (such as race and ethnicity) as well as financial factors (such as class).

sociologists: people who study human society and how it operates.

spectrum: range.

stability: the sense that things will stay the same.

stereotype: a simplified idea about a type of person that is not connected to actual individuals.

stigma: a judgment that something is bad or shameful.

stressor: a situation or event that causes upset (stress).

traumatic: something that's very disturbing and causes long-term damage to a person.

variable: something that can change.

INDEX

Page numbers in *italics* refer to photographs or tables.

advice 27–28, 34

African Americans 24–25

anxiety 15, 32, *33*

arrest *10, 12,* 13–15

bail 15

Ban the Box campaign 43

Bibas, Stephanos 24

Coates, Ta-Nehisi 24

congregate system 22

depression 15, 32, *33*

Dickens, Charles 23–24

employment, convictions and 41–43

incarceration

   children and 17

   costs of 28–31, 35

   critiques of 23–24

   dealing with 27–28, 32–33, 34, 40

   definition of 11, 13–15

   history of 20–23

   numbers of people 14, 19–20, 24, 33, 34

   racial disparity and 24–25

   rates of 19–20, 34

jail 12

   numbers of people in 14

mandatory sentencing 19

mothers 16, 27, 31–32, 34–35

parole *36,* 37

phone calls 29, 30

police *10, 12, 13,* 15,

prison 12–13

   numbers of people in 14

restrictions on felons 38–39, 41–42

solitary system 21, 23

visitation 29, *31*

voting, convictions and 38–39

ABOUT THE AUTHOR

H. W. Poole is a writer and editor of books for young people, including the 13-volume set, *Mental Illnesses and Disorders: Awareness and Understanding* (Mason Crest). She created the *Horrors of History* series (Charlesbridge) and the *Ecosystems* series (Facts On File). She has also been responsible for many critically acclaimed reference books, including *Political Handbook of the World* (CQ Press) and the *Encyclopedia of Terrorism* (SAGE). She was coauthor and editor of *The History of the Internet* (ABC-CLIO), which won the 2000 American Library Association RUSA award.

PHOTO CREDITS

Photos are for illustrative purposes only; individuals depicted are models.
Cover: iStock.com/Montian Noowong
iStock.com: 6 Mordorlff; 9 Den Kuvaiev; 10 Yuri_Arcurs; 12 Pamela Moore; 13 KelleyBoreson; 16 Joe_Potato; 29 Fertnig; 30 Bastiaan Slabbers; 31 Bastiaan Slabbers; 36 StockSolutions
Library of Congress: 18 Carol M. Highsmith; 21
Shutterstock: 26 Larisa Lofitskaya; 33 wavebreakmedia; 39 Andrey_Popov; 40 Waddell Images
Wikimedia Commons: 23